A laid-back
book of
Harmony
Don't even
consider starting
the day without it

(chill, baby!)

Author: Jane Purcell
Managing Editor: Simon Melhuish
Series Editors: Lee Linford and Nikole Bamford
Design: Alan Shiner
Illustrations: Gary Sherwood
Additional contributor: Christine Pountney

Published by:
Lagoon Books
PO Box 311, KT2 5QW, UK
PO Box 990676, Boston, MA 02199, USA

ISBN: 1-904797-55-5

www.thelagoongroup.com

Printed in China

A laid-back

book of

Harmony

Don't even

consider starting

the day without it

(chill, baby!)

One of the kids dyed the dog pink while the others were industriously using your laptop as a sandwich toaster. Meanwhile, the washing machine was busily spewing its contents across the kitchen floor and the dog was contentedly sharpening his teeth on one of your brand new shoes - the ones that weren't such a bargain. Your mother-in-law decided it was a good time to call and witter on about her blighted cabbages and the family Christmas seating plan, whilst the courier, with an urgent parcel from Kuala Lumpur, left (with the parcel) before you were able to answer the door.

It's only 8am. That means there's plenty of time for the day to deteriorate and a very good chance that it will. It also means you're late for the monthly Monday morning management meeting, which is both a mouthful and generally a pointless waste of precious stressing time.

All sounding a little too familiar? If so, this book was written for you. Yes, YOU! Packed with ingenious ways to relax and chill out, by day or night, it's an indispensible commodity for maintaining your sanity in a world that continuously devises new ways to snatch it from you.

We advise that you carry this book with you at all times - we cannot accept responsibility for the outcome should you happen to leave it at home or anywhere near the dog.

Contents:

EARLY MORNING BLISS

Not a 'morning' person?

Here are a few ways to make getting up
(a little) less painful...

Keep the window ajar.
Adequate fresh air means that if you wake up with a
stuffy nose and thick head, it's down to riotous living,
not inadequate ventilation. Even in winter, open
the window slightly and throw on an extra
blanket if you feel the cold.

While you're still horizontal, take a long, unhurried stretch.
This has two major benefits: not only can you delay the
evil moment of getting up, but research has also shown
that the spine shrinks by up to three inches
in a lifetime. If you want to walk tall as an
octogenarian, keep stretching.

When you finally manage to prise yourself from the
duvet, roll onto your side and sit up slowly. If you jerk
yourself upright, you could easily strain your
neck or back.

Once you're up, have another luxurious stretch
to get your circulation going.

WEIGHT IN VAIN

Stop weighing yourself first thing in the morning.
Why should your mood for the day be dictated by a
tyrannical set of scales? Hide the smug little monster
in the back of the closet and go by how
your clothes feel instead.

Instant weight loss program.
(Eat what you like; lose pounds in minutes.)

SHOWER POWER

Get up a few minutes earlier and enjoy a peaceful shower without the rest of the household banging on the door.

Buy a shower radio, turn the music up and sing yourself awake. So what if you're off-key? The shower will (hopefully) drown you out.

Hide some ludicrously overpriced lotions and potions just for you, and refuse to share them. You're worth it.

Impose a house rule: the first person up chooses the radio station and nobody is allowed to change it to Headbanger FM.

THE GREAT OUTDOORS

If you have a garden, or even a small yard, go outside and take a few deep breaths. Get into the habit of feeling your ribs moving in and out so that you're not just breathing in your upper chest.

In warm weather, walk barefoot on the grass. The sensation is wonderful and gardens smell at their best first thing in the morning.

Hang up a bird feeder. Birds will realize very quickly that there's a new 24-hour take-out in town and to watch them swooping down for a quick snack can be extremely therapeutic.

Mad Moose Deluxe Birdfeeder™.
(Coming soon to a bird feed store near you.)

HAMMER HOUSE OF HANGOVER

If you've had a big night out and don't happen to be among the lucky few that can drink indefinitely and wake up as fresh as a daisy, then it's worth being prepared.

Bear in mind that the drinks that cause the greatest morning-after pain have the highest levels of toxic additives.

In order of hangover horror - most offensive to the least - consider your tipple before heading to the bar:

Brandy

Red wine

Dark rum

Sherry

Beer

White wine

Vodka

Mixing your drinks may seem like a great idea at the time but you'll probably end up feeling very sorry for yourself the next day.

Mad Moose Norwegian Tequila™: 98% proof.
(NB: also powers most modern automobiles.)

HAMMER HOUSE OF HANGOVER

If you've stuck to white wine or vodka and still wake
up with a tongue like a well-worn chamois,
all is not lost. Here's what you should do:

Alcohol depletes the body of Vitamins A, B6, and C.
Take a multivitamin and drink lots of pure fruit juice.

❧

A can of tomato juice (Vitamin C), a banana (complex
carbohydrate) and an Ibuprofen tablet (your head hurts)
will help bring you back to life.

❧

Avoid coffee. It may contain caffeine, which will help
your headache, but it will also dehydrate you further.

❧

Drink some flat cola - ideal for an emergency sugar hit.

❧

If you can face stepping outside, get some fresh air -
exercise helps to metabolize the alcohol.

❧

During the day, drink at least two litres of mineral
water to help rehydrate your body.

Complex carbohydrate.

PULL A SICKIE WITH STYLE

Some enlightened bosses are incorporating 'duvet' days
into contracts of employment. If you're unfortunate
enough to be working for a Scrooge, here's the
best way to turn a sniffle, or a hangover,
into a DIY duvet day:

Phone in as early as possible, preferably as soon as you
wake up. Not only is it more considerate, but your voice
will still have that authentic early morning croak.

❧

Make sure you speak to someone who can be
trusted to relay the message.

❧

Briefly state your symptoms.
Be specific. Don't just whine: "I don't feel well".
If the listener is sympathetic don't ramble on about how
many times you had to get up in the night - the more
you babble, the guiltier you sound.

❧

Screen all your calls. You don't want to be caught
answering the phone in a cheery voice only to find the
Personnel Manager on the other end of the line.

❧

Go back to bed.
And if you do feel guilt ridden, just think
of all those unpaid hours of overtime
that you've worked.

*Warning: extended sick leave can
lead to severe exhaustion.*

BREAKFAST BOOST

Take time to eat breakfast.
Too many of us eat 'backwards' by skipping breakfast,
grabbing a sandwich for lunch and having a late dinner.
A piece of fruit and some cereal or toast will help to
prevent your blood sugar from crashing later in the day.

If you really can't face eating, take an apple and a
banana to work, or a handful of nuts and raisins.

Train your partner/kids/dog to help clear up in the
morning. Why should you have to rush about like
Snow White, making beds and washing up? You don't
have to yell, just let them figure out that if sports gear is
thrown on floor, that's where the sports gear will stay.

PRESSURE DROP

Own a pet, preferably one with fur.
Not only are they glad to see you when you
get home, but stroking a friendly animal helps to
lower stress levels and reduces blood pressure.

Many people who don't own pets improvise.

COMMUTER CALM

COMMUTER CALM

17

COMMUTING

If your bus isn't in sight, walk to the next bus stop for some extra exercise, air and natural light. At the current rate of traffic congestion, you'll probably be moving faster than the bus anyway.

☯

If your journey is only a few miles,
consider getting a bike and cycling to work.

☯

Have a chat with the people you normally see on the way to work. That doesn't necessarily mean sidling up to nervous strangers on the train, but a quick conversation at the coffee shop, or with the guy you buy your newspaper from can get the day off to a good start.

☯

Try making use of your commuting time by listening to language tapes. You could pick up the basics of Italian or Spanish for your summer vacation.

Tennis ball infamous for beating London traffic.

MUSIC THERAPY

Carry a personal stereo with you to tune out
from the commuter rush.

The National Academy of Sciences published a study
revealing that music taps into the same brain structures
as food and sex. Although, unlike food and sex, music is
not technically necessary for human survival, it does
activate the same reward and emotion centers
in the brain, making you feel good.

Other health benefits of music include:

Alleviation of stress and anxiety.

☯

Helping to reduce agitation caused
by work stress or road rage.

☯

Releasing of muscle tension and mental tension.

☯

Improving immune system function.

Music also elicits an automatic relaxation response.
If you are listening to Chopin's Nocturnes, your pulse will
slow to match the tempo of the music. Needless to say,
thrash metal is likely to have the opposite effect.

NOISE THERAPY

If you're driving to work and stuck in traffic, wind up the windows. Then scream your head off. Really give those lungs a good blast. You may risk looking a bit odd to other road users and passers-by, but you'll feel a whole lot better for it - and that's what counts.

Anonymous trio performing
jazz-funk rework of
'tie a yellow ribbon 'round the old oak tree'.

HARMONY AT WORK

HARMONY AT WORK

22

Harmony at work.

STRESS FACTORS

What is stress?

Stress is defined as a physical, chemical or emotional factor that causes bodily or mental tension.

We all get stressed out, but the key is to learn how to recognize it, reduce it and manage it.

One of the major causes of excess stress is overwork. Most of us are working longer and harder than ever before in a work culture where job insecurity is endemic.

illegal stressbusters.

If you have one or more of the following symptoms
you could be suffering from stress:

Headaches

Sleep disturbance

Difficulty concentrating

Poor organization

Sense of humor failure

Overreaction to minor frustrations

**Using alcohol, cigarettes or drugs
to 'numb' stress**

**Frequent colds - a sign that the immune
system is under strain**

The signs of overwork may be obvious to your
colleagues if not to you. You may not realize that you're
reaching the point of burnout until someone
remarks that you've lost a lot of weight
or look very pale.

PRACTICAL STRESS BUSTERS

Learn how to prioritize.
Accept that your in-tray is never going to be
empty, but that you can divide it into
three piles in order of importance.

☯

Talk to a friendly colleague who understands
the way the company works. They may be able
to put your work problems into perspective.

☯

Delegate. Winston Churchill was a master of the
art and it didn't do his credibility any harm.

☯

Learn to say "No". If you always accept more work than
you can cope with, lazier colleagues won't appreciate
you any the more. And when you're carted off with a
peptic ulcer, they're unlikely to feel guilty. They'll just
look around for another willing fool to exploit.

☯

Some people run away from an unsatisfactory private
life by burying themselves in work. If you are regularly
working more than 48 hours a week for reasons
other than financial, perhaps it's time to look more
closely at relationships and life outside of work.

☯

Finish one task rather than half-doing three.
The feeling of achievement can be a reward in itself.

Impractical stressbusters.

POSTURE PERFECT

Good posture is instinctive in small children.
They sit and stand without placing any strain on their
backs. Unfortunately, years of slouching and poorly
designed chairs can lead to restricted breathing,
stiffness, headaches and potential back injury.

Good posture is often a reflection of how you feel
about yourself. If you stand tall and relaxed
you will exude confidence.

The good news is you can relearn good posture -
the principle is very simple. Effectively, you should keep
the three natural curves in your back (neck, chest
and lower back) balanced, whilst standing,
sitting or lying down.

SITTING COMFORTABLY?

Sit right back on the chair, not perched on the front.
Pull the chair in, so your fingers can comfortably reach
the keyboard. To prevent lower back strain, put a towel
or cushion between your lower back and the back of
the chair. If your feet don't reach the floor, rest
them on a footrest or a box. Ideally, your
desk should be level with your navel.

Your computer monitor should be at eye level. If you
have to keep looking up or down, it can strain your head
and neck muscles which may lead to headaches.
Get up from your desk at least once every
hour to stretch your legs.

If your back hurts, visit a registered osteopath as soon as
possible to identify the source of the problem.

STAND TALL

Aim for the 'neutral spine', maintaining the natural curvature of your back. We're not intended to stand ramrod straight, whatever you were made to believe at school.

Keep your neck long with your chin softly in (i.e. not sticking out like a chicken impersonation).

Gently pull your shoulders back and down.

Pull your stomach in without straining.

Distribute your weight evenly between the heels and balls of your feet.

Your ears, shoulders, hips, knees and ankles should be 'stacked' in a naturally straight line to achieve good posture.

Strong stomach muscles help to support your back. Yet another reason to persevere with those sit-ups.

Actual examples of very tall men.

FAST REFRESHERS

While you're sitting down, rock about in your seat from time to time or change the position of your feet.

Keep a bottle of mineral water at your desk and take frequent swigs. The body is 70% water; symptoms of dehydration can include bad breath, headaches and lethargy.

Brush your teeth and spray your face with a water mister.

In hot weather, run your wrists under the cold water tap - this will help to cool your entire body.

Try to take short breaks.
Have a chat with a colleague over a cup of coffee.

Take your lunch break away from your desk.
Even if it's only half an hour, eat a sandwich and go for a quick walk.

The lighting in office washrooms is deliberately designed to make you look as if you are on death's door. For inner harmony, avoid looking too closely!

Marcus once held a senior management role.
Whilst taking a rare but welcome break in the park to eat his
sardine and pickle sandwiches he was kidnapped by a rogue
traveling circus, brainwashed and forced to juggle for
18 hours a day. After 3 long years, Marcus escaped.
He now entertains farming families in Iowa.

3 MINUTE CHILL-OUTS

Close your eyes to rest them and take
a few deep breaths.

❧

Curl your hands into tight fists and 'fling' out the fingers.
Repeat this action a few times.

❧

Lift your shoulders up to your ears,
hold for a second...and drop.

❧

We carry a lot of tension in our faces. Try relaxing your
face with the yoga posture, "Lion". Screw up your face,
open your mouth as wide as possible and thrust out your
tongue as far as it will go. Maintain this pose for a few
seconds and then release. Best to avoid doing this during
a meeting or in a supermarket line-up!

❧

Find a quiet spot and stand upright with your feet hip
width apart. Breathe in and as you breathe out, slowly
fold your body forwards, keeping your knees slightly bent.
Don't bounce, just slowly bend forward until
your upper body is hanging loosely. Take a few
deep breaths and very slowly come up,
vertebra, by vertebra. Your head
should come up last.

Proficiency in Japanese:
not a recognized 3 minute chill-out.

BODY LANGUAGE...

You may be smiling and nodding at your boss, but if your hands are clasped behind your back and your eyes are flicking towards the door, your body is saying: "I'd rather be having my teeth pulled than be listening to you." Here's a quick guide to non-verbal behavior and its interpreted meaning:

Brisk, upright walk.
I'm confident.

☯

Sitting with legs crossed, foot kicking.
I'm bored.

☯

Arms crossed.
You'll have a hard time convincing me.

☯

Walking with hands in pockets, eyes down.
I'm fed up. Nobody loves me.
Everybody hates me. I think I'll go eat worms.

☯

Hand to cheek.
Hmm...I'm thinking about this.
(Or I'm trying to cover up a big red zit.)

...AND ITS MEANING

Touching nose.
**Whatever I say, I'm lying through my teeth;
don't believe a word.**

❧

Sitting back with hands clasped
behind head, legs crossed.
**I'm confident. I've got a better job and a
bigger car than you. In fact, I'm an arrogant...**

❧

Open palm.
I'm open and sincere.

❧

Pinching bridge of nose, eyes closed.
**Negative evaluation or
"No I am not going to give you a pay rise."**

❧

Tapping or drumming fingers.
**I'm not even bothering to hide how impatient I am.
Go away you annoying little weasel.**

❧

Patting or playing with hair.
I'm feeling very insecure. Please like me!

HOW TO LISTEN...

The art of conversation is at least 50% listening.
That's why the biggest bores in the world are those who
are more interested in pontificating than in hearing
what anyone else has to say.

Active listening involves concentration, attention and
receptive body language.

Concentration
Focus your attention on what is being said.
Not just the words, but the ideas and
feelings behind them.

Attention
Think of attention as visual concentration.
Lots of people tune out, and just say "Really?" and
"That's great!" thinking that they're doing a fine
cover-up job, but it's always obvious in their eyes.
And they usually get caught out.

It can be more than a little embarrassing if the speaker
says something like: "...he died last Tuesday." and the
listener responds with a standard line from their
repertoire such as "That's great!"

...AND BE RECEPTIVE

Receptive body language

Pay attention to body language. If you lean forward
a little and focus your eyes on the person, the message is
that you are paying close attention. Nodding and
saying "Hmm" helps although you should avoid
looking like a crazed nodding dog.

If you're sympathetic to the speaker, your body will
respond automatically, subtly copying their posture.
If the speaker crosses their legs, after a moment do
the same. You don't have to play mirror games
but the speaker will feel that you're open
and receptive to their comments.

Body language: study the signs.

HOW TO BE ASSERTIVE

Being assertive is not as scary as it sounds. It's simply about making yourself equal to other people.

Check your body language. Nobody will treat you with respect if you shuffle about, head down, apologizing for your existence.

☯

Shake hands firmly.

☯

In meetings, a good strategy for assertiveness (and staying awake) is to decide what you want from the meeting, have a few ideas written down, state them openly, and then listen carefully to what others have to say. You are then in a good position to reach a practical compromise.

☯

Don't shout. Teachers who have to cut across the chatter of thirty students learn that pitching their voice low cuts through more effectively than yelling.

☯

Most people speed up their speech when they're nervous or angry. Make a conscious effort to slow down. The people who carry real authority in their voices never speak like a runaway train.

Retired drama teacher.

HARMONY AT HOME

HARMONY AT HOME

Harmony at home:
not always a pretty sight.

FENG SHUI BASICS...

Feng Shui (pronounced fung shway) is the Chinese art of placement. 'Chi' is the life energy flowing through your environment. Feng Shui looks at how this life energy is affected by the positioning of items within a room or building.

For a sense of inner harmony, you should consider the map of eight forces (The Bagua) within your home. According to Feng Shui principles, any changes you make to improve the chi in a particular area of your home will also influence the corresponding area of your life.

*Chi Chi: exceptionally
chilled Panda.*

...AND THE BAGUA

The Bagua is an octagonal map that overlays a room, your home, or working environment, dividing it into sections. Each section relates to a key area of your life. The segment at the centre of the map influences health.

By attending to specific areas of the chart you should, in theory, be able to improve your life in the corresponding area (listed below). You enter the 'Career' section of the chart if you enter a room or building through a centrally located doorway. The sections rotate in a clockwise directon from your left as you stand in the doorway:

Career & direction

Knowledge & skills

Family

Wealth & prosperity

Fame & reputation

Love, relationships & marriage

Creativity & children

Helpful people & friends

Health (centre of room)

Use The Bagua to place furniture and items in your living or working space to optimize the flow of chi. If the top left (wealth) corner is full of old newspapers and rubbish, it could, according to Feng Shui, explain your whopping overdraft and lousy pay.

CLEARING YOUR CHI

Take a weekend and have a thorough clear out.
Get the family to help you. If they moan, say that you'll
clear out on their behalf and throw away anything you
don't like the look of. That should get them moving.

Say "No" to knick-knacks.
Life is too short to dust a china shepherdess.

Throw out anything broken - the things you keep
intending to fix but never do. Even if it doesn't
improve your chi you'll feel better for it.

Ensure that everything in your house is either useful,
beautiful or gives you pleasure. If it doesn't fulfill any of
these criteria, out it goes. You may wish to mention
this to your partner too!

Be like Attila the Hun and pillage your wardrobe. Get rid
of those impulse buys, the orange flares you might fit into
one day and the hand-knitted sweaters that make you
look like a potato sack. Your clothes should fit
and flatter you, whatever your size.

Once you've purged your house, give it a clean.
And remember - the less clutter, the easier
a home is to keep clean.

CREATING POSITIVE CHI

Chi should be balanced, moving neither too
swiftly nor too slowly.

House plants with round leaves attract positive chi.

A water fountain is one of the best chi-attractors. If you
need a helping hand with your career, place it
in the career corner of the room.

The area around the front door should be clear and free
from trash or outdoor shoes. The theory is that chi flows
into the house through the front door. If shoes are left
there, the chi collects their smell, bringing sickness into
the house. So, no more stinky boots by the front door!

If you have a long, empty hallway the chi could be
moving too fast. You can fix this by hanging a
mirror on the wall.

Hanging a wind chime at the top of the stairs can
prevent chi flowing too fast down the stairs and
out through the door.

Beware! A mirror placed opposite the bed can
attract a third party into a relationship...

FLOWER POWER

Treat

yourself

to a mammoth

bunch of flowers.

Add a spoonful of sugar

to the water to

help them stay

fresher for

longer.

Random bunch of Roses.

HOUSEWORK CRAZY?

Women with jobs spend up to 30 hours a week cleaning. For men this is a far more sensible 14. This is not to say that men should do more, merely that women should be doing a lot less. A harmonious home doesn't necessarily have to be a spotless one.

☯

Children raised in disinfected homes are more prone to asthma and eczema. Our obsession with living in a germ-free environment could potentially create strains of super bugs, resistant to existing medicines.

☯

Remember that housework is essentially pointless because it's never finished. For true harmony, let your housework maxim be "it'll do" rather than "I can't see my face in that floor yet".

Rare picture of a dust mite party.

ANTI-HOUSEWORK TIPS

Many houses are untidy simply because there's a shortage of storage space. If things are hidden away, you'll spend less time charging around with a duster.

❧

Invest in good lighting. It hides dust
far more effectively.

❧

Nobody needs ironed bed linen or underpants.
If they do, they know where the iron is.

❧

Emptying waste paper baskets, picking things up off the floor and plumping up cushions make a room look instantly tidier and are all much quicker
than vacuuming or dusting.

❧

Ignore teenagers' bedrooms. If they want to leave their clothes in a festering heap, that's their prerogative.

❧

Steer clear of your partner's study.
It'll save work and probably conflict too.

KING OF THE KITCHEN

Research has shown that the

more a man cooks, the less

likely he is to go bald.

The reason

for this is that feeding

people produces a chemical

called lexitocin, a sex hormone

that stimulates hair growth!

Many famous chefs disguise impressive bouffant hairstyles with exceptionally big hats.

BREATHE STRESSES AWAY

Relaxed people breathe slowly and deeply from their abdomen. When we're under stress, our heart rate increases, our breath often becoming shallow and moving to the upper chest area. Victorian women frequently fainted, largely thanks to their whalebone corsets which prevented them from taking in deep breaths. This led to constant shallow breathing and a lack of oxygen.

Try the following to enhance your own breathing:

Sit down in a quiet, comfortable place.

Observe the rhythm of your breathing. As you become more relaxed, your breathing will slow down.

Put your hand on your stomach. As you breathe, feel your stomach moving up and down. Aim to breathe from your stomach instead of your upper chest.

Note how long it takes to breathe in and out. If it takes five seconds, slowly increase it to six. Don't push or strain. The idea is that, with practice, you can gently slow down your breathing and feel increasingly relaxed.

*Avoid breathing exercises in the presence
of these nasal enemies.*

UNLEASH THE KILLER Bs!

Nothing is funnier than an unintentionally hilarious movie. Rent some of the worst movies ever made and spend the evening choking on your pizza.

Some killer classics for trashy nights in front of the TV include:

Planet Nine from Outer Space
Polyester-clad aliens invade earth in a cardboard spaceship. They have the technology to raise the dead, but are easily defeated by a firm punch.
Voted the worst movie of all time.

Wild Women of Wonga
An ancient civilization of women with inexplicable access to full make-up and leopard print swimwear.

It Conquered the World
An oversized, power-crazed pickle strikes terror into the hearts and minds of mad scientists and blond starlets.

...and there are plenty more where these came from.

If you get bored with dubious plots, horrendous acting and unconvincing costumes, why not try making your own home movie. Hours of fun can be had.

*Remake of a long forgotten
cult bee movie.*

MEDITATION

The purpose of meditation is to still the mind and attain a relaxed, heightened awareness. It can seem quite difficult at first because everyday thoughts and worries tend to crowd in.

With regular practice, you'll be able to concentrate with far greater ease. Meditation will leave you both serene and alert.

Ideal times to practice are at the beginning and the end of each day. Once you find a time you like, stick to it.

Sit upright, but comfortably, in a cross-legged position, or in an upright chair. If you like sitting on the floor but your back needs some support, sit against a wall. You can't expect to still your mind if your body is contorted.

*Meditation can be done in many places;
some are more suitable than others.*

DO IT WITH YOUR EYES CLOSED...

The real challenge when shutting your eyes during
meditation is not falling asleep!

Seat yourself comfortably.

☯

Close your eyes and concentrate fully on your breathing.
If thoughts creep in, which inevitably will happen,
observe them and let them pass.

☯

Breathe slowly and deeply, gradually increasing
the length of each breath.

☯

Build up your routine to ten minutes each day.

☯

Meditation takes time, so don't get cross with yourself if
half-formed thoughts or worries keep floating around
your head like driftwood. Passively observe them
and let them drift on by.

☯

Get up slowly to avoid dizziness.

...OR OPEN

Meditation can just as easily be done with your eyes open, as long as distractions are minimal.

Place an apple or a lit candle on the floor in front of you.

Seat yourself comfortably, on the floor or on a straight-backed chair.

Concentrate fully on the object placed before you.

When other thoughts wash into your mind, observe them passively and let them pass.

Gently bring yourself back to the object of your meditation.

Build up your routine to ten minutes each day.

Get up slowly to avoid dizziness.

MOOD ENHANCERS

A few aromatherapy tips...

Aromatherapy has been used to enhance mood for thousands of years. You don't have to believe in its reputed healing qualities to appreciate that a few drops of scented oil on a candle or in your bath can soothe and calm your senses after a draining day.

For a stuffy nose, add a few drops of eucalyptus or tea tree oil to your pillowcase, or to a bowl of boiling water.

For insomnia, try a few drops of neroli blossom or sandalwood oil around your bed.

For headaches, a few drops of undiluted lavender oil dabbed on your temples can relieve the tension.

For anxiety, use clove, cedar wood and sandalwood.

For exhaustion, cinnamon and pine should help to revive you.

Most neat essential oils are extremely strong and should be diluted in a carrier oil such as almond or wheatgerm.

*Upon discovering the insomnia-relieving properties of
neroli blossom oil, Gloria moved to Spain and became
the proud owner of a fine orange grove. During her brief waking
moments she tends to it with the care of a nurturing mother
whilst listening to her favourite Van Morrison song.*

COLOR YOUR MOOD

Colors have a powerful effect on our mood.
Even if you're skeptical about the idea of color therapy,
you would probably agree that few people could relax
in a bright red bedroom.

You can make a difference to your everyday life by
decorating rooms in colors conducive to
the mood you want to achieve:

Red
A powerful energizer and stimulant.

Orange
Symbolic of energy and joy.

Yellow
Symbolic of the mind and intellect.

Green
The color of balance and harmony.

Blue
To promote calm and harmony.

Violet
The color of spirituality.

By using different colors in different rooms around
the house you could help to enhance your mood
in varying ways. Relaxation in the living room,
concentration in the study, harmony
in the bedroom...

*Beware: artistic temperament may
result from a color therapy overdose.*

MOOD LIGHTING

If you don't have time to redecorate your entire house purely for the sake of harmonious living, then the feel of a room can also be influenced by using light from colored candles:

Orange
To help create a vibrant party mood.

Pink
For a romantic dinner setting.

Yellow
To encourage conversation and debate.

Green
To restore harmony and calm.

Blue
To release tension.

GET (LEGALLY) HIGH

Inside every person is a store of happy hormones called serotonin. When released, they give you a real buzz and help to prevent or fight off depression.

The most effective way to achieve a serotonin rush is through regular exercise. Find an exercise that you enjoy; one that both increases your heart rate and fits into your lifestyle. Aim to exercise three times a week in thirty minute sessions.

Too busy? If you've got time to watch TV, you've got time to exercise. End of lecture.

Amateur scientific studies recently revealed that it takes 138,229 channel changes using a TV remote to burn off calories equivalent to three well executed sit-ups.

NATURAL HARMONY

NATURAL HARMONY

Harmony 'au naturelle'.

SOOTHING SOUNDS

Some of the most relaxing sensations can be experienced for free. The profusion of sounds that nature surrounds us with are prime examples:

Listen to the waves rolling onto the beach.
If you live too far from the ocean to get a regular dose, borrow or buy a sounds of nature CD - there are a multitude available.

☯

Walk through a forest and listen to the wind whistling through the trees, rustling leaves as it breezes past.

☯

Take a walk in the park and tune in to the crunch of leaves and twigs under your feet.

☯

Listen to the elemental power of a thunderstorm or the sound of heavy rain pattering on the roof or the ground.

☯

When the storm is over, and if it happens to be during the daytime, go outside and listen to the rattle and chatter of the birds on a worm hunt.

SIGHTS FOR SORE EYES

Tired of staring at dreary concrete cityscapes?
Look to a natural remedy:

Put some space between you and urban living. Head for
the hills or mountains and soak up the sensation
of wide open space.

Lie on a beach and mull over the clouds. Watch them
merge into different shapes. Staring at the sky on
a beautiful day can be almost hypnotic, but
don't forget your shades and sunscreen!

Plant some daffodil bulbs in autumn and wait for
a sea of cheerful yellow in early spring.

*We are currently fighting litigation brought about by a man
who became lost in this forest for some 29 years.
Please note: we cannot accept liability
for such incidents.*

SENSATIONAL SMELLS

There's more to life than pollution, fumes and the smell of greasy fast food joints. Get your nostrils working on some rather more refreshing nasal sensations:

Go for a walk after a thunderstorm and breathe in the clean, damp air and the smell of wet earth. Thunderstorms also ionize the air and make it smell lovely and fresh.

Grow herbs on your windowsill or in a window box and occasionally catch their scent wafting through the house.

Take a trip to the coast and breathe in the salty tang of the sea air.

Head for the countryside on a crisp, autumnal day and fill your head with the smells of woodland foliage and the occasional whiff of woodsmoke from cottages with woodburning stoves.

Roast some chestnuts for a warming winter aroma.

Place fresh cut flowers in your hallway so that their scent drifts as you breeze past.

OH, WHAT A FEELING!

Stimulate your body to help stimulate your mind:

Walk barefoot in dewy or wet grass.

☯

Give your feet a massage by walking barefoot on the beach. The sand acts as a natural pumice.

☯

Build sandcastles or stretch out and clench your hands in the sand.

☯

Try snorkeling or scuba diving and experience the rich variety of color and movement under the water, comparable to entering another world.

*Slow protest against clumsy
people with big feet.*

TRAVEL STRESS-FREE

TRAVEL STRESS-FREE

GREAT ESCAPES

It can be more restful to take short, frequent breaks than one long summer vacation.
(If you can do both, even better!)

If you live in the city, try to get out of it as often as possible, even in winter. Go for long walks in the countryside or by the sea for an invigorating change of scenery.

On vacation, there's nothing wrong with wanting to lie on a beach, but at least once in your life, take an adventure holiday. You could learn to ride, go whitewater rafting, or tour Peru by motorbike.
Away from your normal domestic routine, you might just get in touch with your inner daredevil!

*Anonymous man holidaying
in an unidentified location.*

TRAVELING BY PLANE

A few pointers for a more pleasant flight:

Wear loose, comfortable clothing. If the flight is overnight, take a change of clothes to freshen up.

Always take an extra layer. Planes tend to have over-enthusiastic air conditioning and the curiously thin blankets provided are rarely sufficient to keep you warm.

Request a bulkhead seat or a seat by one of the emergency exits. They offer more legroom.

If there are two of you, reserve the aisle and window seats. The middle seats are the last to be sold, so there's a reasonable chance you could end up with an extra seat. If not, the person in the middle will usually be happy to swap seats with one of you anyway.

Stretch and move your arms and legs as frequently as possible to keep your circulation moving.

CUT DOWN ON JET LAG

Studies have shown that flying westwards causes less jet lag than flying eastwards, but you can also reduce the effects by following a few simple guidelines:

When you board, set your watch to local time at your destination.

Avoid peanuts - they cause water retention.
Eat fruit instead. Carbohydrates help you to sleep, and airline food is packed with them.

Cut down on your alcohol intake. At 35,000 feet the effect of a hangover is doubled. Drink lots of water to stay hydrated and go easy on coffee and tea.

Get up and move about as often as possible.

If you can, try to sleep until the breakfast time of your destination.

Take a neck pillow. If you do manage to get some sleep it should help to avoid waking up with a cricked neck.

TRAVELING WITH KIDS

Give your child a light meal before you set off. Provide snacks like plain biscuits and crackers during the journey.

Travel sickness may be a problem. It is caused by motion upsetting the balance of the inner ear. To reduce the effects, afternoons and evenings, as opposed to early morning, are recommended as better times to travel.

If the travel sickness is very bad, your doctor may be prepared to prescribe an antihistamine, which should help to lessen the nausea and make your child sleepy.

Speculated quantity of additional luggage Marco Polo would have needed, had he traveled with kids.

KIDS IN CARS

If you frequently travel with your children by car, get them used to personal stereos unless, of course, you prefer your journey accompanied by tinkling nursery songs at full volume. Story tapes are particularly good for keeping them entertained.

KIDS IN FLIGHT

When you fly, push for a bulkhead seat. You might stand more of a chance with a small child in tow.

Bring a favorite toy or blanket that your child associates with sleep. If that doesn't work, be sure to pack a bag of cheap toys that you can bring out every hour or so.

Pack food that won't run or spill all over the person sitting next to you. Child meals provided are very often evil smelling concoctions, even in Business and First Class.

Have some sweets for them to suck on at takeoff.

Try to keep your child off the fizzy drinks. A dehydrated hyperchild at 35,000 feet is not a pretty sight.

TIPS ON GETTING AN UPGRADE

Ask. A cliché, maybe, but if you don't ask, you don't get.

Upgrades are more likely to be given if you
look reasonably smart.

Be cheerful and polite with the check-in staff. After a sea
of miserable faces lugging their suitcases, your smiling
face might just earn you a bigger seat.

You're more likely to get an upgrade if
you're traveling solo.

A Barclaycard survey revealed that men are more likely
to be given upgrades than women; the perception
being that men are the employers and women the
employees. Which century are we living in?

Most airlines give frequent flyers the chance to
buy a reduced rate upgrade.

If you frequently stay at the same business hotel, they
may offer airline upgrades as part of the package.

Business Class, 1874.

WIND DOWN & CHILL OUT

WIND DOWN & CHILL OUT

Relaxation is a state of mind.
According to Mauritanian mythology it is
also an undiscovered village with a
populus of Lilliputian proportions.

SWEET SENSATIONS

Chocolate is good for you.

It's a fact!

Good quality dark chocolate

(with 70% cocoa solids)

contains beneficial antioxidants,

iron and magnesium.

So get stuck in!

And if you want to feel even better

about stuffing you face with confectionery,

buy some fair trade chocolate.

WINE DOWN

Enjoy a glass of wine even more - buy big wine glasses
and...wait for it...fill one half full. This traps more
of the aroma so you can really savor the
full bouquet and flavor of the wine.

This is Bernado.
Grapes destined for some of the finest
French wines pass between his toes each year.

THE RELAXATION POSTURE

A yoga posture called The Corpse is a great way
to wind down at the end of the day:

Find somewhere quiet, loosen your clothing and
lie down on a firm surface.

☯

If your back hurts, place a pillow under your knees
so that your back is flat on the floor.

☯

Starting at the top of your body, screw up your face for a
few seconds, then release. Move down to your:

Neck • Shoulders • Right arm and left arm
Right hand and left hand • Stomach
Buttocks • Thighs
Feet and toes

☯

Concentrating on one area at a time, scrunch it up
and release. When you've released your toes,
relax completely for a few minutes. Your body
should feel completely free from tension.

☯

When you get up, roll onto your side, onto your knees
and stand up slowly to avoid dizziness.

Relaxed man painting relaxed moose.

BATHTIME BREAKS

If you have a small child, use their bath time as a chance
to catch up on a bit of non-strenuous pampering.
Sit with your feet in the bath and give yourself a
manicure or a foot rub.

Ivor Tightthong.
Available for foot massage while you
attend to routine household chores or the
needs of your children.

BOOGIE TIME

Close the curtains,

turn on the stereo and dance

about to the kind of disco music

that made the 1970s

the decade that taste forgot.

Get those hips moving and gyrate like

it's gone out of fashion.

And make sure you're alone!

BASIC BACK MASSAGE

You don't need any special techniques to give a relaxing massage. If your partner doesn't have any back problems, all you need is some oil, a comfortable surface and a warm room.

Before you start, your hands should be warm and the oil should be at room temperature. Any scented oil will do, but almond is particularly good.

❦

Kneel at the upper left side of your partner. Pour some oil into your cupped palm, then gently apply it all over their back. Mould your hands to the contours of their body.

❦

Place both your hands at the center base of your partner's lower back, with your fingers pointing towards their head. Push your hands towards their neck, keeping your palms flat. Then move your hands in opposite directions out and over the shoulders.

❦

Bring your hands down again to the base of your partner's back and repeat this four or five times. This movement is called effleurage.

❦

Add more oil if necessary and keep your movements smooth and flowing.

Rudulfo - Bernado's brother.
Boasts 25 years experience massaging
the feet of grape crushers. Also does backs
but requests that you bring your own olive oil.

INSOMNIACS CORNER

Only use your bedroom for sleep and sex.
It may sound obvious but if your body associates the
bedroom with work, you'll find it considerably
harder to switch off.

❧

If you eat late, go for starchy carbohydrates which
actually help with sleep. A biscuit can trigger a sugar
low during the night which may wake you up.
Slow releasing complex carbohydrates,
like pasta, are far better.

❧

Avoid nicotine or coffee in the evening.

❧

Sleeping pills may work to break the cycle
of insomnia but their long-term use
can become addictive.

Sleepless in Skegness.

BATHING GLORY

It's almost impossible to feel stressed out in a warm bath.
Turn yours into a mini-spa by doing the following:

Make sure the hot water tank is full.

Tell partners/children/housemates/the cat/
your mother-in-law that nobody is allowed
to disturb you unless the house is
burning down.

Lock the door and light some candles.

Use a scented bath oil such as lavender
which is very calming.

Read a trashy novel, the kind you wouldn't
normally be caught dead with, even on the beach.

HAIR HORRORS

If you go to bed with hair like a movie star and wake up with hair like a caveman, try sleeping on a slippery satin pillowcase.

Satin causes less friction than cotton, which means your hair takes less punishment while you're asleep.

Mad Moose Hair Trauma Support Group™:
caters for all your follicular counseling needs.

WRITE STUFF

Keep a journal. Writing down your thoughts and feelings can be very therapeutic.

Don't censor your handiwork, just put the ideas down as they come into your head. Not only can you gain a perspective on problems, but journals are very useful to look back on. Just make sure your journal is well hidden from prying eyes!

It has been said that Shakespeare penned 'A Midsummer Night's Dream' during his sleep.

BETWEEN THE SHEETS

Choose a firm mattress. If you're stuck with a saggy one, slide a board underneath it.

Lie on your side with your knees slightly bent towards your chest.

If you lie on your back, place a pillow under your knees to support it.

Sleeping with more than one pillow under your head can exaggerate your neck curve and place undue strain on your back.

Follow your dreams...

Keep a separate notebook and a pen by your bed for some DIY dream therapy. Dreams that seem astonishingly vivid on waking, usually melt away by the time you've staggered out of bed. Write your dreams down and they will do one of the following for you:

Provide a fascinating insight into your psyche.

Give you a good laugh.

Convince you that an urgent appointment with a therapist is necessary.

Other titles in this range include:

**A very useful book of Magic Spells
to help you get everything you ever wanted
(without much effort)**

**A very useful dictionary of Dream Analysis
explaining everything you ever wanted to know
(but didn't dare ask)**